T0195069

MEMORIES

My Story of Redemption

Brenda Murray, LPC
Marialena Ward, Editor

authorHOUSE

AuthorHouse™
1663 Liberty Drive
Bloomington, IN 47403
www.authorhouse.com
Phone: 833-262-8899

Published by AuthorHouse 02/08/2021

ISBN: 978-1-6655-1355-5 (sc)
ISBN: 978-1-6655-1353-1 (hc)
ISBN: 978-1-6655-1354-8 (e)

Library of Congress Control Number: 2021901091

Print information available on the last page.

This book is printed on acid-free paper.

KJV – King James Version
Scripture taken from the King James Version of the Bible.

CONTENTS

ACKNOWLEDGEMENTS

To Karen, my longest and dearest friend, I knew that when you read my story that your thoughts would be well thought out, loving, and honest. Thank you for taking your time without hesitation and providing guidance. My appreciation and love for you goes on and on!

To Renee, at the time I showed you the "67 Memories," I did not know why God chose that time for me to share them with you but I certainly know now. The series of events that ended in this book were driven by that meeting and the trust you had in me to be a "speaker" at W.O.V.E.N, which God has entrusted to you to make sure it glorified Him. What an honor you bestowed on me. Thank you.

To Emily, even though I have known you the least amount of time, I am in awe of the trust I have in you. You are wise beyond your years. We had many face to face times together and you helped me to "speak" the story out loud, sometimes with tears but always with prayer, gentleness, and patience which made it so much easier. You have continued to support me in many ways along this journey and I cannot thank you enough.

I love you Em.

AUTHOR'S NOTE

When I began to write "My Story" it was to share it with all of my family. I believe they don't truly know about how I grew up, what happened to me, and the joys and sorrows that I experienced. That is my fault because I grew up not sharing. I want them to understand some of the people they have known in a complete and truthful way, including myself.

However, this story has developed into something else along the way. It has morphed into a story of redemption in the life of one person. I am not sure how or where it will end. It is important to me that whoever reads "My Story" will gain something from it that gives them new ways of seeing how the tragedies that we suffer can be turned into triumphs. That when God says, "all things work to the good for those who love him and are called by his name," (Romans 8:28). He means it. I have learned that sometimes it takes a long time for us to grow into maturity, understanding, and acceptance. But if you are willing to look closely, you will find how many of the hurts and tragedies have been redeemed in countless ways and that you have already been compensated for the faults or bad aspects of something that has happened to you.

Please note, that this book does not contain all 67 memories only the most noteworthy events are captured in this story.

INTRODUCTION

There are many people who have helped me see and receive God's compensation. As strange as it may seem, some of those people are the very ones who caused me pain and sadness. For without them, I would not know the goodness of God and I would not know what victory feels like.

Additionally, there are those who have loved me through some of my most difficult times. Friends who taught me how to express my feelings, those who knew my faults and insecurities, yet have all loved me anyway. My children loved an imperfect mother and made me smile many times with their warmth and affection. Recently, there have been those who have listened as I painfully poured out memories that I had shared in the past with only a very few. They have prayed for me, listened patiently, and never caused me the pain of any judgement.

Furthermore, my husband has had to deal with the aftermath of the things I brought with me into our marriage. How we have made it through 55 years of marriage is a miracle in itself. Somehow, we made it through rough times that I have often felt were caused by my insecurities and fears. I am not saying that he does not have a few quirks of his own but they do not seem to be of the magnitude that mine were. We both would have to admit that the change in our lives happened when we came to know the Lord in November of 1970 that made all the difference. Divorce was never an option that we would have considered. The Spirit gave us the strength and commitment to never quit, to work through trials, and to love.

CHAPTER

THE BEGINNING

I stood behind the podium trembling as I looked out on a room full of women. I knew some but many I did not. All of them had their eyes fixed on me waiting for me to speak. How did I get to this place and time in my life? Was I really going to tell a story never told and were they going to understand? Was it too late to run? I felt like I was experiencing one of those times when your life flashes before your eyes. Only this time...it was the last two years that flashed before my eyes.

About two years earlier, I was enjoying working in the yard. This is something that I still love to do. As I stood in the backyard, I stopped what I was doing to consider a memory that was triggered by something, I don't know what. It was a short memory but a very vivid one. I kept working and in no time at all a second memory came to my mind. I was a little surprised by this one because it was not a pleasant memory but again it was brief. I was reminded of something that happened

1

without remembering the whole event and the feelings that usually accompanied it.

Once again, I went back to working around the yard and a third memory from my past came into my mind. This time, I felt compelled to stop completely to consider what was happening to me. Was the Lord trying to say something to me that I just wasn't getting? I was capable of refusing thoughts that caused me discomfort. I have learned, for the most part, to recognize an attack and quickly divert the thoughts that were not useful to me. If I was going to get more memories from things in my past, many of which I did not want to remember, I had to consider why. If more were to come, then I needed to see them in writing or else I knew I would forget them later. I went inside and got on my computer to type the ones I had already had and think more about them.

Surprisingly, that is not what happened. As I began to put the first memories in my computer, they just kept on coming. The memories came so fast that I could not complete typing one when another would follow right behind. One right after the other, they came like a flood. After about two hours, they finally stopped. In total, I had *67 memories*. Some were warm memories of the friends I had as a child. Other memories were of happy times at my relatives in the country. Most of them were things I had shoved deep inside of me. I had never intended to think about them again. But now I was forced to look at them in more detail. Why?

What would I find after all this time? Would I remember the details of the events? Would I be able to pinpoint and feel the emotions that I felt when they happened? What I did know was that most were painful. I truly did not want to look at them. I knew that in order to not fall apart emotionally, I needed to wait and examine them at another time. So, I put them in my imaginary box for safe keeping and told myself I would look at them later. I quickly forgot all about them which was not an unfamiliar reaction to the hurtful things in my life. I have evaded hurtful memories before but I knew that I couldn't keep from facing these memories sooner or later.

Fast forward a year and a half or so later, I knew that the moment had come and I began to feel the need to share these memories with someone. I called on a woman I had come to love and respect. I felt that I could trust her with my deepest secrets. She and I had met a few years earlier when I was invited to attend a women's luncheon by a good friend. I have never been someone who liked to go to women's meetings. However, I felt I could not keep refusing my friend over and over again, so I went.

I thought of those meetings as boring with a bunch of older women listening to boring stories about their past. I figured I would find myself in the midst of what many of us used to call "Blue Hairs." (When I was much younger the blue hairs were the older women who had weekly hair appointments, the same hairstyle for forty or fifty years, and a tint the beauticians used that caused gray and white hair to have a bluish hue.) Funny how that would intentionally fit right in with the younger generation today. My attitude about going to that meeting was not good. I decided that I would tolerate the meeting and never have to go back.

Watching closely as the guest speaker started to share her story, I began to realize that this was a group of women who met regularly to enjoy a meal, share what God was doing in their lives, and listen to a speaker tell of how she had overcome sorrow and traumas. Immediately, God started speaking to me so loudly that I had a problem staying with what was being shared. What I did hear was a story of almost epic proportions. She had gone through deep emotional pain and a level of poverty that most of us in the room never experienced. But God gave her a miraculous way out that started in her garage and developed into a huge financial success. Then I heard God speak to me in a way He often has. He said, "Brenda did you hear that...did you hear how she glorified me?" I felt like He had taken a ruler and wrapped my knuckles with it. Instantaneously, I realized, God was not finished with His lessons. "Look around Brenda, what to do you see?" He asked. As I looked around the room, I saw beautiful, imperfect women who were spirit filled, who loved the Lord, and wanted to honor Him with their lives.I was feeling just a bit self-righteous in that moment. I think God knew I needed to be humbled a little more and my lesson was not over. He put a new perspective on the situation that I will never forget.

I looked around again and what I saw was a room full of women, many younger than myself. I may not have a blue hue to my hair but I have the same Spirit working in me as these women. Age had absolutely nothing to do with what God was doing that day. The Holy Spirit had everything to do with what was happening in my heart by changing my own prejudices and wrong thinking.

With my new God given perspective of who these women really were, I began to see the immense value in the lives sitting around the room. The Lord definitely tweaked my view on ministry being done in and through women's groups and I am better for it! Since then, I have not only gained so much from many of those women, I have become an active part of that ministry.

CHAPTER

THE FIRST TELLING

Three or four months later, I knew that the moment had come for me to take the memories out of the box and share them with someone. I chose to call on the woman who founded that group. I had come to love and respect her. I felt petrified and excited over the prospect of letting her see my list of *67 memories* but I knew that I could trust her with my deepest secrets.

So over lunch one day, I showed her the list that I had kept hidden for so long. I watched her face as she read them. She looked up only every once and a while to share a compassionate look or to get clarity about one of the memories. The lack of her comments was a little unnerving at the time but I could tell that she understood what I was sharing. When she had finished reading, very little was said, yet she exuded empathy and acceptance knowing how difficult it was for me to share those things. We went on our way that day without discussing the memories any further. I felt so much better afterwards being able to "put them in the light" as the scriptures tell us to do (Mark 4:22). Evil cannot hide in the light. That is one of God's best and maybe most used healing tools. Once in the light, our shame starts to fade and courage to share grows stronger.

Once again, we met for lunch. She shared that the speaker for the next meeting canceled and she did not have anyone to replace her. Jokingly I said, "you can always use me and I can share my *67 memories*." She did not react like it was a joke, instead she said she would pray about it and for me to do the same.

I immediately thought to myself, "Oh Lord, what have I gotten myself into?"

Weeks came and went along with thoughts about that last lunch she and I had together. I thought I was in the clear, until sometime later when she called me to ask if I would share my memories with the group. I did not know what to say. So, I told her I would give her an answer very soon. In trying to decide what to do, my prayers became fervent, filled with both fear and shame that grew inside of me. How would I do what I had initially refused to do...was scared to do for at least 60 years?

A short time after that call, I was in my office looking for a resource book on the Holy Spirit for a client. I stumbled upon a book by John Bradshaw called "Healing the Shame That Binds You." I had never noticed it before. The name was too much of a coincidence for me not to pick it up. I turned it over and read the back of the jacket and knew right away that picking it off the shelf was not an accident. A quote by the author read like this: "I began to see that shame is one of the major destructive forces in all human life. In naming shame, I began to have power over it." As a mental health-substance abuse counselor, I wasn't sure how sharing my story in public would affect me professionally. But the fact that I was a counselor, was one of the things that God used to confirm what I was to do. I had been given my answer.

I contacted my friend and agreed to speak at the next meeting. It would take a lot of prayer, encouragement, and time to put this story together. I needed to decide what I felt comfortable sharing and what to leave out. Who would I talk about in my story and would my words create sadness or trouble for them or their family? My story, like all our stories, involved so many other people. I was not as worried about what my immediate family would think. I knew that even if I upset them, that they would do their best to love me through this process. But what about my relatives and friends who might recognize who I was talking about. Some of them were privy to details and facts. If not, they knew me well enough to figure things out. Would they be disturbed by things they read about someone that they love? Would they think I lied to gain some weird kind of attention or that my memories were confused? I knew what I would talk about and what I would later write about were vivid and true memories of things that really happened. The memories bring with them very real emotions and even body memories of how I felt when they happened. Also, I knew that these experiences are very normal and could be healed in anyone who has gone through trauma. But now, I had the dilemma of how to share the reality of my memories and protect the reputations, lives, and hearts of others. Was that even my responsibility? I have been "protecting" people for years, knowing that many have memories and perspectives of family and friends that are different than mine. Some have developed very loving relationships with their friends and family and have apparently moved on with their lives. Perhaps many would not even remember what I cannot forget.

CHAPTER 3

CLIMBING MOUNTAINS

As I was working through those obstacles about sharing my story, I found some were difficult, but were achievable. This process for me was like climbing mountains. I was barely out of the valley, when I began to see the summit that holds rest and peace. God tells us that we will never have more put on us than we are able to bear but He will give us a way out (I Cor. 10:13).

During my journey through this came a new trusted friend who was willing to listen to my story without judgement and offer encouragement as well as acceptance to me as I poured it all out. I practiced with her several times with tears and prayer until I became more comfortable with hearing myself say the words.

Now there I was standing behind that podium, I couldn't wait any longer to speak to this crowd of women who were already staring intently at me. I began with **"The good and the bad events in our lives**

are often linked in strange ways. There are common threads that are woven through our memories, some happy and some not. The memories are twisted together into long and strong threads that wrap themselves around us and we seldom know that they have become a part of who we are. The strongest threads are those which include strands of secrets and shame. It was like that with me."

I explained further that not all my memories were bad or traumatic. Because of that, it often made remembering difficult. How do you separate good and bad, happy and sad emotions that developed long before your grown-up mind could help you figure them out? I decided that I needed to start with a little background. My knees stopped shaking (at least I don't think my shaking was visible) and my mouth opened. I began (no turning back). I needed to speak.

My mother was two people. No matter how flawed she might have been, she was the matriarch of our family. On one hand, she managed to keep the household together without the presence of my father and little money (mom never held a job that I remember). She was a meticulous housekeeper. Mom was the one who helped relatives in trouble or a friend in despair. Many of them found their way into our home for an undetermined amount of time.

But on the other hand, she drank, sometimes heavily, and I never knew which mother I might find. Unfortunately, that was never far from my mind. Although she had bad judgement at times, she had a

11

good heart. I really believe that I developed a type of sixth-sense about the disposition of my mom. There were times when I would be walking home from the bus stop and I would know to prepare myself for walking into the house. For example, one day as I walked home from the bus stop I had that "oh no" feeling that things were not good at home and I tried to brace myself. When I walked in the door, I saw a woman on the sofa with blood all over her. The blood had soaked the towel in her lap. I looked long enough to see that she had a deep cut along most of her forearm. I don't remember that anything was said but I felt I knew who cut her; someone in the family who did not like her. But nothing was ever said about it again and like the good girl I was I did not tell anyone. Later, I actually believed that I could tell by the sound of the phone ringing when she had been drinking. It was God's grace that helped me to be prepared for most anything.

Regardless, she wasn't a mean drunk, but her values and behaviors would change when she drank. She would scream at my father for not providing enough or not being at home. She would tease me as my body was trying to change into womanhood. That would stay with me well into my adult years causing me to be stuck in a place of shame. Moreover, she behaved in very improper ways with men. Sometimes being so drunk she would forget I was in the room. Once, when I was about eight or nine, I stood and watched as she leaned against a man (I did not know him) as he put his hand down her pajamas. I tried to come between them but was pushed away. I went to my bedroom, my safe place, until I pulled myself together. Of course, this was not something I ever told anyone or mentioned to her. [All of this made me have unhealthy, distorted ideas about what was appropriate behavior with the opposite sex and did not help me to develop a proper self-image. God and maturity helped fix those wrong beliefs. I had no one to teach me how to be affectionate in a healthy way, to hug someone or hold them just because you love them, not because you wanted to make love to them. As time went by, God started to redeem that. He provided very loving people to nurture me and show me a love I did not know growing up.]

Alcohol and the effects it has on people was center stage in the story of my life. Sometimes violence was part of the act. When I was young, I did not realize that good and bad were never far away from each other, especially when there was drinking. I lived on the main street in Lakeside and there was a "beer joint" right next door and another directly across the street. My mother would frequent both and I would often be with her. When I was about four or five years old, I was a very cute little girl with Shirley Temple curls. I was friendly and outgoing from all the reports I have heard. All the grownups in the beer joints loved seeing me come in and I came to recognize many of them. They bought me pie and sodas and would sometimes put a quarter in my hand. I loved the beer joints and being with all the grownups. What I

13

did not know was that not all the people there saw me the same way. One night, my mother went somewhere and one of the men from the beer joint came to watch me while she was gone. I must have seen him before because there was no fear in me. But he took me on his knee and everything changed. He molested me. I don't remember much after that but somehow my mother must have found out because I never saw him again at those old haunts or in my house.

Sometimes the drinking and the friends that came along with it were scary. But other times they were simply pitiful and harmless. For instance, there was Ralph (not his real name), my mom's cousin. Ralph would come to stay with us while he was drinking and inevitably he ended up in the living room chair sleeping and snoring with his mouth wide open. Once my mother thought it would be funny to play a trick on Ralph. She quietly came up to him as he slept and used his mouth for an ashtray. That is not really funny. It is sad. He really was a likeable man and was innocent enough but not exactly who you wanted sleeping and snoring in your living room if you brought your friends home with you.

In addition, there were also those who were a bit bizarre. Rufus (not his real name) looked to me to be a 100-year-old man. I am sure he was not but to a little girl he sure looked the part. I guess I must have impressed him in some way or treated him kindly. I will never know. He was tall and thin. I remember him looking very country as he stood in the doorway to the kitchen in his overalls talking to my mom. I heard him talking about me and that he wanted to take care of me. He even said something about marriage. My blood ran cold but my mother's ran hot. She had him out the door immediately and I never saw him again. Score one for my mother.

However, drinking and my mother's benevolent nature did not always end up being useful at least where I was concerned. Once she had a man who was just a friend but he also drank a lot. She and one of her good friends who was also a drinking partner became worried about him, so we were off to his house to check on him. This was not an unusual occurrence. My mother even had a key to his house. I went into the living room first and there he lay buck naked on the sofa, passed out. I found out how fast my mom could move because she had me out of that house in record time. But it only takes an instant for some things to be burnt into your brain. The image still comes back to me but now I feel sadness for him. I wondered if he ever stopped drinking; if he got his life together; did he ever find redemption, purpose, and love in his life? As I have recalled the events in my life, I realized how blessed I am to have found all those things.

As I think about what comes next in my story, I am thankful that while drinking and violence where all around me it never landed on me. I handled violence in many ways. The most common way was to go upstairs to my room and shut the door to cry for a while.

At the time, it was my safe place. I seldom told anyone that I cried nor did I tell anyone about the events that took place in my home. When you are young, you don't know what goes on in other homes. It sometimes takes awhile to figure out what isn't normal. But some things teach you fast about what should and shouldn't happen in the life of a normal family. By this time, I was a teenager and my mother had been seeing this man who seemed to be one of the "okay" guys in her life. One morning I came down the steps and the two of them were in the living room. He was standing there quietly while my mom was on the sofa. Something didn't feel right and she did not look up at me as I came down the steps. I slowly walked over to her and when she did look up her face had been badly beaten. It was swollen, bloody, and bruised. She did not say a thing, no explanations. They both just remained silent and I retreated to my room again.

She eventually married him and they remained married until she died. Overtime, I came to appreciate him, but never really felt close to him. As for my mother, even in my adult life, when my father-in-law died, she came to the gathering after the funeral, drunk. She embarrassed me by loudly telling everyone there that I was avoiding her because I was ashamed of her. She was right! She continued doing that most of the time she was there, it felt like an eternity.

Later on, my mother became a physically unwell woman. Her lifestyle and her choices caught up with her. She needed a dutiful daughter to help her through the very hard times she faced. I was the only caregiver she had for a long time. Actually, I felt I was good at it. I don't know how I got to be good at being a caregiver. Maybe, it was a sense of responsibility; maybe, I felt sorry for her; maybe, I knew that she did not have the means to hire anyone; maybe it was love.

None of it was easy because of my emotional wounds but it served as good training. God used those tough times to create in me a much needed servant's heart. For the most part, that gift remained in me and I am very grateful for it. Once again, God used His unique talent of turning the events in my life. I could have traveled down many different paths. I could have been bitter, hopeless, judgmental, or many other things that often lead to death of a soul. Instead, I traveled down a road that led to Him and life.

On top of everything I had been through, I became the person responsible for taking care of her husband when he developed Parkinson's Disease. I had to find somewhere that he could be as comfortable as possible on what income his Social Security, pension and modest savings afforded; until it ran out. Not an easy task financially for him or emotionally for me. God's grace sustained me when "duty" was not enough reason for me to continue. It was sad, he had no other family and few, if any, friends came to visit. In the end, he died a hard death and I was glad that I was able to care for him. Giving comfort to others is not restricted to only those with whom you have a good relationship. God tells us to "do good unto ALL men..." (Galatians 6:10)

CHAPTER 4

PLACING BLAME

Even though I wanted to do good, I blamed my mom for my father not wanting to come home when I was growing up. As a little girl at the age of ten, I came to understand that my father was also leading two lives. He was a kind, gentle, laid back, and generous man. Also, he was extremely smart and ingenious. But he had no desire to "make it big" and that drove my mother crazy. He invented a new spooling system in the DuPont Nylon Plant with almost no reward except a pat on the back. That invention was in the plant for years until the nylon plant burned down, or so I was told. As far as I know, DuPont never rewarded him because of a contract they had with employees at the time and it became just one of those things. Even if he was offered a promotion, he turned it down if it meant taking on responsibilities outside his regular duties or working longer hours. He was not lazy; he just marched to the beat of a different drum and getting ahead did not seem to be a priority to him.

I never saw him drink, even a little. But he was absent from our home and mostly from my life. What a strange thing for me to adjust to, my father always sober but hardly ever home and my mother who was always home but hardly sober. My father demonstrated gentleness and quietness but I seldom got to see it in action and my mother demonstrated anger and bad behaviors that I got to see often. Which one is the bigger influence in a child's life? Does a child make a decision at some point which one to trust or to let be their example?

I only heard my dad curse one time. He came home early one day and found my brothers across the street behind a fast food burger stand. They were having a confrontation with a neighborhood gang. Someone had a gun and at some point the gun went off. No one was injured. My father picked up my brothers by their belts and pulled them out of the fray and sent them home. I had no concept of "God's Hand" at that point in my life but later I would come to understand how His hand was in what happened that night. Just the fact that my father was available that particular night to change what could have happened makes me think of divine intervention.

When I think back, I remember being about five years old and we were somewhere in downtown Richmond standing outside on a hill. My dad picked me up and looked at me straight in my face. He asked,

"Brenda who would you rather live with? Your mother or me?" I had no way of understanding what he was really saying. How could I answer him? For me there was only one answer. I looked him straight in his face and said, "Both!" Later, I came to blame him and his absence for mom's drinking. As a child, I guess I thought someone had to be blamed. As an adult, I wondered if he was trying to take me out of what was often a chaotic environment with my two brothers getting into teenage trouble.

At first, I thought that my father was not at home because he worked two jobs. His day job was at DuPont and his night job was at the Broadway Drive-In Theatre. He was an usher. He was the guy who walked around the theatre making sure everything was going along smoothly and folks were enjoying the movie, not just each other. Often, he made trips to the back of the theatre parking lot and would shine his flashlight into car windows. Surprise!

My friends and I liked this job. It was a great thing for us because we could go to movies a lot and they had live country music on most summer nights. I saw Minnie Pearl and Grandpa Jones one night…so cool. My friends and I would sneak out of the theater and make our way to a nearby farm. We had learned some time before that this farmer grew delicious watermelons. So we would pick one and high-tail it back to the theater. There, we would break it open over one of the benches on the playground and dig in. It was messy and left us sticky but it was so good. Those escapades into the melon patch ended the night a shotgun went off. The farmer didn't shoot at us but he put the fear of God in us and watermelon raids became a thing of the past which was just another memory that made us smile.

Because he had to stay until the last car left the theater, I would often fall asleep in the back seat of my father's old Plymouth. Many times I would wake up at home in my bed the next morning and he would already be gone again. But one night I woke up, it was dark and we were not at the drive-in. He was not in the car. I peeked out of the window but I did not know where we were. I became scared, so I hid under the old army blanket he kept in the car because everyone knows that "if I can't see you, you can't see me." It felt safer. After a while, dad came back to the car and I pretended I was still asleep. I never let him know that I was awake and I certainly did not tell my mom.

I don't know how many times I fell asleep in the back seat of that old Plymouth. However, one of those nights when I had fallen asleep, he woke me up and took me into a strange house. He sat down and put me on his lap. He introduced me to a woman I had never seen before and several sleepy-eyed children who looked as perplexed as I was. I lowered my head not saying anything. What could I say? They were the reason he worked two jobs and they were the reason he was gone all the time. Even a little girl could figure that one out. This was his other family. I don't know what my mom knew at the time but I never said anything to her. I did not tell anyone until it became obvious years later. I still don't know what my brothers knew but I began to realize that there was a lot of blame to go around.

As an adult, knowing all that I know now, I understand why he asked me who I would rather live with. He wanted to take me away from my mom to live with his "other family". Even to this day, I am unsure of how I would have responded if I had known what he wanted to do. On one hand, it brought reassurance that he loved me but on the other hand, I could not have left my mother. I did love her despite the many bad things she brought into my life. It was like she really couldn't help herself.

I spent a lot of my time thinking about the other family who had my daddy most of the time. That came back to haunt me when he passed away. In preparation for his funeral, I sat with the other family as we shared things about him to help the person doing the service. I heard them sharing and laughing about the joy of vacations together, many funny stories about the quirks he had, and many other things about him that I did not know. I had little to add so I quietly got up and left the room.

Thankfully, the experience of hearing their memories of my father that I was not a part of was redeemed through his death because I got to know that other family. I would have never had that opportunity otherwise. I saw their love for him and how they were trying to get to know me. They were actually nice people who wanted to know me better and I had not been making it easy on them. By getting to know them, I found that several of them shared the same love for the Lord that I have. For the first time in years, I was able to let go of the jealousy and wrong perceptions. I allowed relationships to form. We are not close but there is no longer animosity in my heart.

I can't leave the subject of my father without letting you in on the best kept secret of them all. I used to tell my kids when I would catch them doing something that they knew wasn't right, "You know God will bring the wrong to the light in the strangest ways." I had hoped that they would think twice about what they were doing, the things that they thought were unseen and that had gone unpunished. God allowed that principle to be used in my life in 1980.

I had been having some health problems and the doctor found I was anemic. No matter what she did, it was not getting better. She decided to send me to a hematologist to find a way to evaluate my red blood cells and correct the condition quickly. I was told by this specialist to get blood samples from my children and both of my parents so he could do a comparison test to see if what he suspected was true. If the same blood condition was found in their samples then that would prove the doctor was right in his suspicions. Samples were taken and we found two of my children had the same condition that I did. It is called Thalassemia.

Earlier I told you, "I actually believed that I could tell by the sound of the phone ringing when Mom had been drinking?" This was one of those times. I had been trying to call her and my father about setting up a time to get the test done. When the phone rang, I just looked at it because I knew she was drinking and I didn't want to answer it. But I did answer it and I was right. She was slurring her words but they were clear enough to hear her say, "You don't have to get a blood sample from your father." I told her that was the only way to confirm the blood disorder by comparison. But she insisted, "You don't have to ask him because he is not your father." I felt my knees go weak and the room start to go dark as she was trying to explain. I heard myself say, "I don't want to know about it," and I hung up. I broke down which brought what was the first of many tears. Except in the beginning when the hurt was fresh, I seldom brought this up except with the closest of friends. The way I shared about growing up, after learning that the father I had known was not my biological father, drastically changed. I tried not to share anything for fear of exposing my "real" childhood and the convoluted mess it was at times. So much shame was still alive and well in me. [I thought I had grown past all of that but because I have a heavenly Father who knew me before I knew him and He is redeeming the hurts in my life, much of the hurt and shame has been taken away. I have been able to leave this battle to God and his timing. (2 Timothy 1:12-14)]

Even so, the doctor had enough samples to determine that I had the Thalassemia trait. The way I understood it is that some of the blood cells were mis-shaped and did not attach to other cells as they should to get the job done. This is similar to Sickle Cell disorder. It is Mediterranean in origin. The family origin of the man I always believed was my biological father was German. The major issue is that if anyone with the trait marries someone with the same trait it could be deadly for their children. Two of my children have the trait but they were told to be on guard and test whoever God brings into their lives before any of their children and grandchildren are conceived to avoid a possible tragedy. I was never informed because my parents did not know. So much for "what you don't know won't hurt you." But again, I had been blessed in my ignorance because the man I married did not carry the trait.

It was several years before I found out who my biological father was. It happened only as a result of a friend convincing me that I would regret it if I did not find out. My tendency to not tell things sometimes manifested itself into "don't ask". She went with me to the home of the man I knew as my father to plead with him to tell me the name of my biological father. I don't know why he did not want to give me his name, maybe that was somehow part of his shame. Maybe he thought I would think less of him. I wished that I had assured him that as far as I was concerned, he was my father. He died not long after he told me. God's timing, I guess.

5

CHAPTER

A VERY LONG WALK

By now, most of my shaking had stopped and I looked around the room. Women were still intently listening to my story. I thought that was a good thing. I noticed that the noise of clattering plates and sporadic chattering had ceased. Maybe it was time to tell a lighter flavor of the story before I shared the really hard stuff.

"Not all memories were bad," I heard myself say. My best memories were of the times when I would go to visit my grandparents (my mother's parents) in the country. They were better known to me as Big Mama and Big Daddy. They lived in a big white house. As I have gone back to visit it as an adult, it no longer fits my current definition of "big" but it looks the same from the outside which evoked wonderful memories.

It was a two story framed house that was modest in every way. It sat on a relatively small piece of land but had a large garden area in the back of the house and a barn behind that. The property extended for several hundred yards beyond the barn and ended at the creek. They owned a small horse that someone gave them because he had a deformed nose. His name was Tom. He looked like someone had hit him in his face with something and left his nose very crooked. We rode him and he went very slow. We could not make him go fast until he turned around and saw the barn...then it was "hold on for dear life!" For us kids, he was part of a dream playground. Their house had no heat upstairs. So they used big, heavy, handmade quilts on all the beds. The only heat source came from one space heater in the living room and a wood stove in the kitchen which doubled as a stove for cooking. In the winter, you could stand next to the space heater in the living room until you felt as if your backside would catch on fire. Then, run as fast as you could upstairs and jump under the quilts. That worked well. For years they had an outhouse that served for the warmer months and daytime needs. In the winter, there were thunder mugs or chamber pots which served to meet those necessities of life. Eventually, they added a bathroom with a tub onto the porch. But again, no heat and you had to run across an open porch about 15 feet to get there. Bathing was an exhilarating adventure!

Speaking of adventures, my love for working in the dirt came from those visits. My cousins and I would help in the garden. To make it fun, we made a game out of digging potatoes. The one who dug the most out of any hill of potatoes won bragging rights. My cousins cheated or so I thought. My Big Daddy gave us a little money for the task and we went to the county fair which was held at the old Rockville school. This was the school my mom went to and happened to be the same school that became the ballfield where my grandchildren played little league for years. There were good memories there of cake walks, greased pig contests, sack races, and bobbing for apples. Or we took what little money we had and walked to the store in Oilville collecting bottles for a refund along the way. Our reward was as much candy as our money bought. It was a long walk. By the time we got back to Big Daddy's, most of the candy was gone.

My cousins, the neighborhood kids, and I often played in the barn which was off limits during bailing season but that would not stop us. We climbed on the hay bales all the way up to the rafters and once there, we skidded across the rafters to scare the guineas away. Not the cleanest game considering the guineas left their droppings all over the rafters. We did not care, after all droppings washed off. The best fun was jumping down from hay bale to hay bale with dust and hay flying everywhere. Until, one day Big Daddy caught us. He was standing in the door and an even larger shadow was cast across the barn floor. Evidence in the form of dust and pieces of hay still lingering in the air could not be ignored. We were in trouble. We did not try to wiggle our way out of this one. He was a man of few words and just the fear in his presence was enough to scare the misbehavior right out of us.

However, he was a gentle and dependable man. As an adult, I

learned that much of who he was came from his trials and his faith in the Lord. It was evident to me when Big Daddy was in the hospital battling tuberculosis. He was able to teach me from his wisdom without saying a word. On one of my last visits with him, I sat holding his hand and praying. He was in a coma and I did not know if he knew I was there. I felt God urging me to sing to him. That was something I was not comfortable doing if I thought someone may hear me. No one was in the room and I started to cry and sing. Then God did something that I will remember for the rest of my life. I know it was meant to comfort me. As I sang to Bid Daddy from the corner of the room, an image appeared full of light. It was just an image but I know who it was or who had sent it. The light faded after a few moments but in my spirit I had no doubt that somehow my grandfather was aware of it too. [It is not wasted to talk or pray with someone who appears to be in a coma or unconscious. There is even power in a touch. God takes care of how that is perceived by the person. Our job is to show them love and compassion.]

When I was around ten years old, something upset me at home. I had to get out and go somewhere that I felt safe. I decided to run away to my refuge, the big white house. So, I packed a small bag and started my journey to Vontay where my grandparents lived which was 23 miles away. There was a light rain for most of my journey but it did not bother me and it helped wash away the tears that I tried to control but couldn't.

I walked up Broad Street for over eighteen miles. I came to Shallow Well and needed to take a right turn to leave Broad Street behind. As I turned and started walking towards Vontay, a truck stopped and a strange man rolled down the window. It did not take a genius to figure out something was wrong with me. He asked where I was going and when I told him he said he knew Big Daddy. He offered me a ride the last 5 miles of my quest. [Now I know what you are thinking... "don't get into the truck"] But I was a ten-year-old little girl who was soaking wet and exhausted from walking for almost nineteen miles, all I thought about was getting to Big Daddy's. I was not thinking what might happen to me. Now I know how stupid that was but I also know that God can cover us with His grace, protection, and mercy in spite of our stupidity. The man took me straight to that big white house and I believed I had won that battle. However, my grandparents called my mother and I returned to Lakeside the next day. I didn't get punished, but we never talked about it again that I remember which was typical in our house. The whole thing just got buried and nothing really changed. [Children will sometimes go to great lengths to feel safe. Especially, when they feel unable to control anything in their world. God was with me that day but I did not realize it until many years later. If we could only see how often God protects us from harm. Meanwhile, we never knew it was Him controlling the situation.]

While in the country, I had some of my earliest encounters with the Lord. My grandparents always went to church and we got to ride in the back of their woody station wagon. Those were the days when you could ride in the back with the back window open and look out. Life seemed to always be a game or competition to us in the country. My cousins and I counted the frogs on the road, whole or flattened, as we made our way. The church was a little framed building. Out back, most of my relatives on my mother's side of the family were buried there. Attendance on a good day was maybe 75 or 100 souls. Most of them sang loudly and off key. I hated Sunday School because the teacher made us do sentence prayers and I did not know a thing about any kind of praying because religion was not a valued activity in my home. By the time the prayer came around to me, my sentence had been used by someone else. Unfortunately, I ended up without a prayer and I was embarrassed. [Funny how life goes full circle. I am now deeply entrenched in healing prayer and prayer counseling. I am never embarrassed but honored to do so. I believe that is something that was redeemed in my life. Since about 1980 until this day, I have gone through many classes and seminars dealing with prayer and praying. Even my skills learned in counseling have added to the way I minister prayer to folks. God does indeed redeem the things in our lives and remakes them if we cooperate.]

Also, in the country I learned that persimmons that were not ripe would turn your mouth inside out. My cousins tricked me. On a walk down to the creek, we passed a persimmon tree and they convinced me that the persimmons were really good. They had faked biting into one, so I followed and did the same. I felt like my whole mouth became one giant pucker! There was nothing that I could do to stop it. They laughed loud and hard at me for a long time. In the fall, when the persimmons have turned orange and are starting to fall off the tree is the time they are ripe and can be picked.

I found such security and quiet love from my grandparents. I had so many friends who lived around them and I don't remember one time feeling shame, fear, or anger during my visits there. The big white house was a refuge for me. I wished more than once that I lived there all of the time.

The country memories were the best, but most of my life was not lived in the country and the "fun" memories at home, in Lakeside, were very different. These memories are a bit scattered yet interesting to recall. For example, my brothers were like Butch in "Our Gang Comedy" or "The Little Rascals." Butch was the tough guy who today would be identified as the bully of the neighborhood. On a walk with a friend, we were harassed by a carload of boys and it scared us. But one of the boys recognized me as being the sister of "Bubba." I heard one say "hey, don't mess with her I know her brothers," and they left. My friend and I shared a kind of bravado that was instilled in us from having older brothers. Our older brothers commanded respect from many of their peers.

In the city, we had fun doing things like climbing up the walls of an unfinished building after the workers had gone home. We jumped into the piles of sand they had neatly left to use the next day. One particular building, a liquor store in Lakeside, was our "playground" and we did not allow others to play there. One day, another neighborhood kid tried to be a part of our fun and I ended up fighting him. I won. That is not anything for which I was proud, but I was a tomboy so by default it was what I had to do to keep my reputation. Later that evening, there was a knock at our door. That same kid and his father were standing there as I opened the door. I had bloodied this boy's nose and his father was mad. Now I felt ashamed about the humiliation he must have felt as his father came to face his attacker, a girl. That incident did something to me that grew into trying very hard not to embarrass anyone. When I became a Christian and started to learn about forgiveness, I was not able to even remember his name in order to find him.

It was also there that my brothers introduced me to my first cigarette in the alley behind our house when I was about eight years old. They convinced me that I needed to take a deep drag and swallow. I got so sick I never smoked after that; they didn't know it but they did me a favor. [I believe that God was using them to teach me something that I would not have learned any other way. (Romans 8:28)] I never took up smoking after that day which was another good thing out of a bad deed.

Another random memory was of a birthday party where I hid in a locker behind the garage while playing the game hide and seek. My head quickly found a wasp nest and I was stung thirteen times on my face. I ran into the house after being stung screaming my head off but my mother was in a serious discussion with a social worker. She was there to check up on my brothers who seemed to always be in trouble. I could tell that she did not know what to think of the situation. My mother seemed to handle my hysteria well. I can't imagine what the social worker thought. My father was told and he took me to the emergency room. The doctor told me I would need a shot and I held out my arm. "No" the doctor said, "the shot will have to be given in your bottom." Even at that young age while I was in great pain and my face was grotesque looking, I would not let him approach me. I had enough sense to know that I would have to pull down my pants in front of him and my father. I was just too modest for that. Nothing was worth that to me. I jumped off the table before they could stop me and started to run. My father and the doctor had to chase me around the table, but I did not succeed in escaping. The trauma of exposing myself to them that day caused me to feel a shame and embarrassment still felt to this day. To make matters worse, my lips were so swollen they touched my nose! My eyes were swollen shut and I had to sip my ice cream through a straw.

One of the weirdest memories was living next door to a recluse. We lived next to a lady who we rarely saw in daylight. As kids, we called her the "crazy lady". She pruned her bushes at night and I heard the branches snapping right under my window. When my friends and I played in the street, sometimes our ball went accidentally into her yard. It was always a race to see who got to it first, her or us. If she won the race, the ball was never seen again. As years went by, I heard pieces of her story. Her son had died a tragic death. The deep grief she developed changed her. After that, she never wanted to leave her house during the day. I am embarrassed to even share that we, as children, did not give her the respect and understanding she deserved. [As a counselor I now know how important that is. We do things that follow us for a long time and sometimes we cannot go back and fix it. We can only find forgiveness from the Lord.]

Also, there was a honeysuckle bush in the vacant lot next to our house. It was the biggest honeysuckle bush I had ever seen. It was so big we were able to create a door and carve out the inside while the outside still looked normal. For a while, this was our "neighborhood clubhouse." It so happened it was near an alley right behind a restaurant. We hid in that bush when we saw the man delivering drinks to the restaurant. We waited for him to go in with his order. He left the side of the truck open because he was only gone a few minutes. We rushed out, grabbed some drinks, and threw them in the bushes. Then we scattered until the truck was gone.

That didn't last too long because the truck driver got wise to our trick and when he went into the store, he watched for us to do our crime. He came running out of the store yelling at us. We all scattered and he never caught any of us. But, we never did it again. We were much too smart for that. It was the end of our free drinks but it was the beginning of seeing that God has a way of making our misdeeds known. [When my children did things they knew were wrong and thought I did not know, I often had already been told by someone about the deed. I would surprise them with my all-knowing powers by bringing it up to them. Then I would tell them, "God sees what you do and when we think no one knows, God has a way of making our misdeeds known." I sometimes used that to try to bluff them into confessions but that seldom worked.]

Because woven through all of the good and bad memories were broken threads that damaged the cloth I was made of, I developed feelings of hate, loss, shame, and embarrassment. God would have to reweave the cloth of my soul. [I think you will see what I mean as I share with you the rest of the story about the honeysuckle bush.]

As a young child, I had many fun times hiding in that bush with my friends. We did daring, mischievous things and did not get caught. (Well maybe sometimes we got caught.) It felt like a safe place, a special place, a secret place but that bush holds within it perhaps the biggest secret I ever had. In that bush before I had even reached my teenage years, I stopped trusting and experienced an abuse that would never leave my memory no matter how far I pushed it down. I was sexually assaulted by a relative and one of his friends. I don't know that I really knew what was happening at the time, but I knew it was not right. I was told never to tell and I didn't, not until I was grown, married, and walking with the Lord. The Lord showed me that there really were people that could be trusted to listen and not judge or be disingenuous. There were people who taught me His love and how to show that to others. To this day, it has remained a secret to most of my family (not including my husband). The struggles that came out of that experience and other abuses served to equip me with compassion and understanding of what others were feeling and the battles that they were fighting.

[I am able to help others with their pain and offer encouragement that tells them that healing is possible but it would become a burden in my marriage. That will have to wait to be told in another part of this story.]

CHAPTER

SECRETS

My mother's family was full of guitar picking, banjo thumping, fiddle playing cousins who loved to have a few while they played. They often ended up in our living room. That was not always a bad thing. I learned to love the music of Earnest Tubb, Grandpa Jones, Minnie Pearl, Flatt and Scruggs, and Tennessee Ernie Ford. I loved Tennessee the most and knew "You Load Sixteen Tons" by heart. At the time, I must have been around eleven years old. I used to think I could play the guitar and sing. I wailed out that song off key on an untuned, very cheap instrument in my room with the door shut. I saw visions of stardom one day. My mother must have thought I was cute because when she was drinking she would force me to perform in front of all her cousins. All of the cousins played an instrument except my mother. I felt that I must have put on quite a show because they laughed and egged me on trying to encourage me against my will. I was dying inside. I hated how that happened and how embarrassed I was. [I probably still remember most of the words to that song by Tennessee Ernie Ford, but if you ever see me please don't ask me to sing it.] Making me perform affected me in a very negative way for most of my life. It robbed me of the joy of singing in front of people. Instead, it created a stronghold in my life.

But again, this was one of those times when the good and bad events were tightly woven together and almost impossible to separate. One of mom's cousins who showed up on a regular basis was Henry (not his real name). He was tall, a little gaunt, and obnoxious. He was almost always drinking when I saw him. He became a memory that brought up anger and shame in me every time I thought of him. Henry was an alcoholic who seemed to show up at our house when my mother was not drinking and would get her started. [If you said that I did not like him that would be an understatement.] He was the only person I ever grew to hate.

It began late one night after I had already gone to bed. I heard a terrible commotion coming from right outside my bedroom door. I opened the door in time to see Henry literally being thrown down the steps by my father. I had never seen my father that angry or that violent. My father followed him down the steps and threw him down the porch steps forbidding him to come back. What I saw next nauseated me. My mother half-dressed, staggering, and coming out of the bedroom across from mine. Soon, I was down downstairs with my mother and father in the living room. I stood to the side like an 11-year-old spectator at a boxing match who didn't belong there. Mom and Dad were in the center of the ring throwing barbs at each other. Each blamed the other. My father exclaimed, "How could you do that with Brenda right in the room next door?" My mother loudly responded, "I needed the money, you are not here and I don't always have enough to pay for everything." My father said, "Why do you drink that way and do these things, you have to stop." Then my mother said, "When are you going to stop?" Both justifying what they had done yet no one paid much attention to me, the spectator. [Tell me, who would you put your money on in this boxing match? Doesn't matter, you would lose. There were no winners.] I retreated to my room. I cried a little and regrouped my emotions.

I never told anyone. [Who would I tell?] Social Services had already been to our house many times in the past because of my brothers' delinquent behavior. I was always a good girl but what would have happened if the wrong people got wind of some of the things taking place in my home. Certainly, there were Child Protective Services back then. If they had found out what happened in our house, I thought we would be taken away. We may have been placed in a home somewhere and maybe not together. Or worse we would have ended up in foster care. The court had already sent my brothers once to live with Big Daddy and Big Mama when they got in trouble. In my heart, I wished I could have gone with them. [Sometimes children have all kinds of fears but the threat of being taken out of the only home they have known may be at the top of the list. There is an odd kind of security in someplace that is home to you...even if it is just one safe room.]

Sometime later, Henry showed up again at our house drunk as usual and not caring about what he was told by my father. The liquor emboldened him. It either made him forget or maybe he never intended to stay away. He loudly knocked at the front door and mom must not have heard him. She did not go to open the door, so I did. I only opened it a little. Just enough that he saw me and I told him he could not come in. I closed the door on him. He continued to knock even louder and told me to get my mother. I went to open the door again only this time I had gone to the kitchen first and gotten a knife. I opened the door and I put it close to his face. I told him that if he did not leave I was going to kill him. He looked down and smirked at me. My mother intervened at that moment and took the knife out of my hand. I am not sure what I would have done if she didn't. I went back upstairs. I did not want to know what might be happening downstairs. [That is not the end of this story...God would use this experience again, much later in my life.]

Years later, as an adult who had been walking with the Lord for a while I was learning about forgiveness. I felt the Lord telling me I had to find Henry and ask him to forgive me for the hate I had felt towards him and the threat I had made against him. I fought the idea for a long time telling the Lord, "no." I did not want to forgive that man and I really did not feel like I needed to have his forgiveness. But the conviction would not go away, and I finally agreed to go "up the country" to find Henry in order to ask for his forgiveness. Before I met with him, he got drunk one night and walked out in front of a truck. He was killed. All I thought was "why Lord did this happen?" "Why, after all the struggle of getting to the point of agreeing with You did you let this happen before I could ask for forgiveness?" [I told God I will never be able to be forgiven for my thoughts and actions toward him.] God's answer to me was clear. [Forgiveness is Mine to give] I just had to be willing to ask Henry for forgiveness. The rest was between me and God. That lesson became part of a teaching that I wrote on forgiveness and had the honor of sharing it. [The idea or purpose of the lesson is twofold: 1. To always remember that forgiveness is not really ours to give. It comes from God through us to others. 2. To realize that we need to learn to complete the forgiveness process we start. It is seldom done in a onetime act of contrition on our part. God will show us how to complete that process if we are willing.]

[By now you should see that my story is all about how good and bad events are often linked in strange ways. When we are able to see how they are linked, we begin to see how God can redeem the events in our lives. None of these events were easy because of the emotional wounds but they served as good training. God used the tough times to create in me a much needed servant's heart. For the most part, that gift remains in me and I am very grateful for it. God used His unique talent to turn the events in my life. I could have traveled down many different paths. I could have been bitter, hopeless, judgmental, or many other things that often lead to death of a soul but instead I traveled down a road that led to Him and to life.

I wish I had known then that the Lord captures every tear I shed and holds them until He turns them into joy. (Psalms 56:8 The Passion Translation)]

CHAPTER

RELEASING SHAME

From sharing my memories, I found that I no longer felt fear or shame and knew that I had gained so much personally. Bad memories seldom leave us but I found that the memories get separated from the pain over time. [It isn't that the pain is gone but it seems to have changed.] In me, it morphed into something more useful. [Maybe it has become strength, or wisdom or empathy. I am not sure. I remember when I had my first child it was very painful but I really don't remember the pain itself, only that it was. We can look at pain differently from outside the event that took place in another time and learn. I know my life is one that is soaked in grace and blessed with redemption. I am who God made me to be and He is not finished with me, nor with you.]

In Joel 2:25-27, the scriptures tell us that God told His people that He was going to restore the years the locust has stolen and remove all shame from them. I knew that is what God had been doing for a long time in my life. At times, it was hard yet at other times I didn't even know He was doing it. [My past will continue to be a part of my life and who I am for as long as I have breath.] I was good at hiding the parts of my life I did not want others to see. Shame worked its power on me and it would take the Lord to untangle it. That is where the rest of my story started.

I never intended to write about the things that happened as I was growing up. [I suppose that is why God gave me 67 memories when I wasn't expecting them. All I ever wanted to do was to forget.] The transition to the rest of my story has been very difficult. However, I have come to value the healing power of truth and not keeping secrets because of shame or fear. I didn't learn about God growing up. [You're not surprised?] I didn't know anyone who called themselves a Christian. All of my grandparents went to church regularly but that did not mean anything to me. I have no memory of them sharing their faith with me until I was grown. Even then, they shared very little. Their faith was private. When I started to go to church, the only song I knew at all was "Jesus Loves Me". I could not have told you what John 3:16 said. But I was always a good and obedient girl trying to do the right thing most of the time.

At the age of 23, I had been married to Phil, my hardworking husband, for 5 years and had 2 small children. God was setting up the circumstances that would forever change my life. We were weekend partiers and did not see anything wrong with hard drinking, things going on in the back room of parties that were not talked about, and watching X-rated movies. I didn't go against the crowd. I wanted to be cool and liked. [I think even before I accepted the Lord he was changing me.] I was becoming disgusted with the things I saw. Many things provoked memories of growing up that I did not want to remember. I had hardened myself against these memories. I was starting to see the danger of staying in that kind of fun. [The kind of fun that will creep up on you until you are entangled in it like being in quicksand.] I saw some of our friends sucked down into addiction, adultery, divorce, beatings, and suicide. [Now I know my disgust was part of God's grace.]

Around the same time, two of our close friends had been converted at a *lay revival* and were looking for sinners. They knew that they had a good catch in us. We were living week to week, almost day to day, and only had one car. On Thursdays, I took Phil to our friend's house so he and our friend could ride together to work. Phil got a spiritual earful on the drive to and from work. I took our car to run errands and I picked Phil up after work. Often, I visited with the wife awhile before leaving to run errands. She was softer but just as relentless in sharing her faith. [We didn't know it at the time but we were snared in a holy trap.]

This couple did not let up! So in order to get them off our backs, Phil agreed for us to go to the *lay revival* at their church one time if they would agree to stop bugging us. The ironic part was that we found out later that the wife had a hidden drinking problem and that they divorced a short time after we started going to church. But, God had used them to bring us to Himself. [God will use anything that seems right to Him to achieve the intended goal. In Numbers 22, He caused a donkey to speak to Balaam about how he mistreated the donkey and that his life was on a reckless path.]

I was a little more willing to do the right thing and go to church for the sake of the children than Phil was. [In case you don't believe, God really does set up the circumstances in our lives.] The night we went the pastor was preaching on the book of Revelation 20:11-15, the great white throne and judgement. [You can read that scripture to see what we heard that night for the first time in our lives.] We were scared to death, about death, at that point and wanted to see what happened next. We came back the next night to hear the rest of the sermon and kept coming. [If you think that life got easier after that, not necessarily so.] We got better but most things in our lives remained the same. We still had financial struggles, a third child coming, trying to remain in relationship with our old friends and make new ones at the same time, and trying to live by new rules given in the Bible that neither one of us knew anything about. Phil came from a stable family and he knew none of the trauma and tragedy I had experienced. He was not raised as a Christian. He was raised as a Catholic in background only because they did not practice their belief. We wanted what we saw in other people;

their values, their commitment, and their personal relationship with the Lord. We wanted to learn more about who this Jesus was.

Phil and I reacted differently to our introduction to Jesus. Phil took off like a rocket. One friend said that Phil needed to be locked in a room for six months until he settled down. He wanted to throw people down the aisle. [Me, I'm a "show me" person. I want to see how things work, what makes a Christian click, and I would question what the Word said. I move slowly in making big decisions, always wanting to do the right thing, and Christianity seemed no different.] I was the tortoise and Phil was the hare. It took a while for me to catch up.

I knew that when Phil and I knelt together asking Jesus to come into our lives that it was real. I knew it then and I know it now. But what I did not know then was what to do with what had really happened to us. It scared me some. I wasn't feeling what those around me seemed to feel. Those who were believers, some for a long time, were excited and shared stories of how they had been healed of so many different things. They talked of joy, love, and peace in the midst of trials. I felt like a phony, just pretending to have what everyone else had. I did not know what was missing. I had done all the right things. We went to church; we were trying to learn about Jesus and His words; we hung around with other Christians but still something was missing. I wanted to know what it was.

Shortly after we became believers, we were scheduled to be baptized.

I had gone to my pastor to tell him that I didn't get the "being baptized" thing. It just seemed like a ritual or tradition. He explained why we are called to be baptized, that it was meant to be an outward sign of something that is an inward change. I still did not understand baptism but he was the pastor and I trusted that he would not lie about what seemed to be such an important event in the church. So being the dutiful, good girl I had always been, I was obedient in being baptized too. I didn't know what to expect, but when I was dunked beneath the water the only thing I felt was wet! I was confused and maybe disappointed that I felt nothing. So, I figured that nothing had happened.

The next morning, after Phil left for work, I sat in my bed alone and I began to ask God about it all. Actually, I began to argue with God about it. [What happened last night? Why don't I feel the things others feel about you? Phil and I are happy, we have all we need: a new house, two healthy children, good friends, the two of us are healthy, so why do we need you in our lives? Where were you when I was a child and I needed you? Where were you when the ugly, painful abuses were happening to me and to my mother? Why do I need you now?] The silence in the room was deafening and I did not speak another word. Then God spoke to me for the first time that morning, but it was not the last time. In a voice so clear that to this day, I cannot say that it was not audible. He spoke my name, "Brenda, that is why you can't see me or feel me the way some others do. I was with you in all those things that happened to you and I have never left you, I brought you to this day." [I know now that God was showing the anger that stood between Him and me.] I cried for a while and thought about all that had happened the night before and that morning. I made a decision that was different from the one I made when we knelt with the pastor and Jesus became our savior. I promised to trust Him in my life even when I doubted or didn't feel Him. In that moment, I made Him Lord. I felt something I had not felt before. [I believe it was His Spirit touching mine.(Psalm 42:7)]

When Phil and I came to know the Lord neither of us really knew what to expect. It was strictly blind faith but it was perfect timing. This happened in the early 70's while the "Jesus Movement" was in full swing. It was a time where anything goes. Some things were not as grounded in sound teaching as it should have been. But then again, we hadn't had very much teaching at that point so it all seemed awesome to us. It was fun! The combination of free-spirited Hippies and new believers full of the Holy Spirit made for a very interesting life. Every encounter gave an opportunity for us and others to grab hold of something new.

However, we were only pseudo hippies though wearing clothes that seemed to work like bell-bottom pants and psychedelic colors. I had hair down to my waist and Phil had a Beatles' style haircut. He wore shirts with very wide collars and bell bottomed polyester pants. We were cool and God did not seem to mind because He guided us into deeper waters with mature mentors. We started to do a street ministry in the Fan District of Richmond (an area near the Virginia Commonwealth University) and that field was ripe with plenty of "real" hippies hungry to listen and sometimes challenge us.

[My best and worst trait back then and now is that I ask questions that sometimes are not understood and hard to answer. I want to know why and have the answers to questions that people do not have the answers to; only God does. It seems so fruitless to say, "why God" because we will either not be satisfied with the answer, will not understand the answer, or already know the answer that we didn't want to hear.]

Having been a Christian for a short while, the woman who became my mentor and my friend taught me a lesson in overcoming struggles that I still try to apply to my life. I had been asked to go to a women's retreat at the church we had just started attending. I had never been to a women's retreat and I was told that the theme of the retreat was going to be LOVE. The thought of going somewhere with a bunch of strangers who were going to seek the Lord and be willing to be vulnerable frightened me. I just did not think that I could do that and listen to stories of how wonderful their lives had been or how they were so happy.

I sought out my friend/mentor and told her why I was scared to go. I asked her what I should do. [Her answer is as clear to me today, almost 50 years later, as it was that day.] She said, "Brenda, you can't fight the battle unless you are on the battlefield." I knew she was right. I called and committed myself to going to that women's retreat. This was to be a battle that I fought more than once. On more than one occasion, I seriously considered changing my mind. A couple of times in my life, I just refused to step out onto that battlefield. [But the battle will continue until you are ready to go where the fight is.]

The battles I have not faced have come to me. I have faced many battles while writing my story. The battle of retracing each memory in order to express it in writing. I had to face the emotions often created by them and decide what to include or how much to include. I wanted to be truthful and share things without dishonoring anyone who may be connected with them. Many of which have been redeemed in my life.

[I am doing that because some of the things may still have an effect on the lives of others. There were times I wanted to suck it all back in, but I can't. I know that there is some self-righteousness in thinking that I have something that may influence the lives of others. It is harder than I thought, it threatens me with shame, it lays me open to what others will think of me, and the questions they may ask. I worry about how it might affect my life and profession in negative ways. I am trying to trust that I am hearing the Lord correctly about this and that sharing is my part in winning the battle.]

Finding and understanding the things that happened to me was to be my quest for a long time as I tried to figure out the events and people who had shaped who I became. I wondered if I would ever be able to accept some of the things that happened to me, things that determined how I felt, how I acted, and how I thought of things and people. [How we speak to ourselves and what we believe about ourselves means something. What we believe about ourselves changes so much about how we feel, how we act, even how we present ourselves to others and more.] As I look back, it seemed only fitting that I became a counselor. I learned not only how to reason things out better but I knew how evil and abuse could actually work for the good in a life. I have seen that happen not only in my life but in the lives of others. (Romans 8:28)

[In life there will always be trials and many opportunities for God to apply His Grace to us with His love and redemptive nature.] I found that God was determined to use me in spite of myself. I have gained so much through loss; the loss of a child and loved ones, loss of friends, loss of financial gain, days when faith seemed loss, and loss of my direction at times.

[Life can be so up and down, and so it was with me. (John 16:33) My husband found one of my journals when we had only been Christians a few years and said of my notes, "Brenda, you sound like David; up one day and down the next." He was right but I don't think I am alone.]

CHAPTER 8

RELEARNING AND REDEMPTION

After a few years, we joined our mentors in a ministry to teach bible studies at the women's prison near us. We barely knew what the bible or the Lord was all about but we went on the coattails of our mentors. It was sink or swim and we learned quickly how to swim. It was great! The demands of the ministry caused us to grow quickly in our understanding of the Lord and the scriptures. Before I knew it, I was praying with the women there and I hoped that I did not look like I had no idea what I was doing. The saying that "God does not want our ability only our availability" became one of my mantras.

God showed us the hearts of women in prison and any preconceived notions we had changed quickly. It taught us lessons about race and gender that otherwise would not have been a part of our world. Going into the prison indeed introduced me to women I would never have met any other way. The vast majority were in prison for their connection with the drug world and all it encompassed. There were women who were in for using drugs, selling drugs, and who were under the control of a pimp. Some were in for writing bad checks because they felt they had no choice [considering some of their circumstances I may have done the same thing]. There was a gentle, wise older woman who loved the Lord and I came to love her. She was in for killing a man. [But when you are functioning on a heart level it doesn't seem to matter.] Most of the women had become hardened by the unspoken rules that controlled the winners and losers inside. One night, I met one of them.

A woman I did not recognize came to the bible study that was being held in the basement of one of the prison dorms. It was not long before it became obvious that she was not there to learn about Jesus but to test us. I was leading the study and I was still a novice. [A novice about to learn a hard lesson.] She raised her hand, looked me square in my eyes, and asked, "Do you smoke?" "No," I answered. "Do you drink?" "No," I answered. "Do you do drugs?" "No," I answered. "Do you go out and fool around with other men (besides my husband)?" "No," I answered. She looked at me with doubt and a smirk on her face and asked, "Just what do you do to have fun?" She looked around the room laughing and hoping to get the same reaction from the other women. She got the reaction she wanted out of them. Suddenly, I felt a fear rising up in me. As I prayed silently, I remembered another time a woman came to a bible study to settle a score with one of the other inmates and brought a knife with her. We found out later that the prison guards got wind of it and took the woman with the knife out of the meeting. I did not know what this new visitor to the class was capable of doing. But I knew, I had to do something. I knew I had to take back control of the meeting that night and quickly. Then God stepped in and gave me the words to say. I looked her square in her eyes until the room became very quiet and still. I teared up and answered her, "I come up here to see you...to have fun." God's love that was given to me for her taught us both a lesson. I saw how strong gentleness can be. [Score one for divine wisdom.] The atmosphere in the room changed and the women started to join in again. That woman never came back. This adventure at the prison became another example of how the good and the bad events in our lives are often linked in strange ways.

We had been going up to the prison for about three years and found that it didn't take as much brains as it did love, commitment, and humility. One night on our way to the prison, as we drove up Broad Street, a two-lane highway at the time, we saw a car coming towards us swivering into our lane. It had a blown out tire. We hit at 55 miles per hour, headlight to headlight. The motor in our car was pushed back almost a foot under the hood. I was knocked out and I don't remember a thing. [My husband remembers it all.] He told me later that he was scared because he thought I was dead. I did not move. He kept telling people around him to pray. I am told the only sentence I spoke was a question about our kids. I asked if the kids were okay. They had not been with us. I must not have believed the emergency responders and in my flailing around I hit one of the volunteers, Cowboy, who I knew. [They would not let me up so I could check on the kids.] I hit him so hard that when he got to the ER they asked if he had been in the wreck too.

When I started to wake up at the hospital, all I could see were bright lights and I felt someone stroking my head. I thought "this must be heaven." It wasn't. It was the lights in the ER and someone was wiping blood off my face and out of my hair. That glimpse of the ER was the only memory of that night that I had. I had a broken back, a deep cut on my chin, and a lot of aches and pains. I did not come home for almost a month. I laid there drugged for most of that time so that I wouldn't move. My back healed completely. I did not have to wear any kind of brace and have had almost no residual problems since then. I was alive and that alone was a miracle.

I had a lot of questions for the Lord after that. [The kind you probably have had at some point. All of those "why" questions for which you seldom get an answer; and even when you do it is usually not the ones you desire.] But this was to become even a bigger lesson about how God links together the good and bad events in our lives.

[As I look back, I see how many of my questions were answered.] I just needed perspective.

One of the first things I learned was that the car that hit us held eight members of an African-American family ranging from an elderly woman to a small baby, no one died. The elderly woman who had been in the car was the same woman I had met just a couple of weeks before the accident while visiting a relative. This was a well-to-do family that had four generations of women living in that home. I had my two-year-old son with me and he was one of the most loving little guys you would ever want to meet. My son went to each one hugging them goodbye. As we were leaving, there was that same elderly woman. She was the maid who was ironing in a little room that we had to pass to get to the front door. My son pulled away from me and ran so fast to her I could not stop him. He wanted her to pick him up so he could hug her good-bye. She looked at me to see if it was alright. Things were different back then and she was quietly asking permission with her look. I would have never refused for my son's sake or for her's. He hugged her tight and she hugged him back with a smile of delight. In that moment we shared... our eyes met. I will never forget it. The connection was very strong at that moment and it was priceless. It was a God thing. It didn't take much for me to see the miracle that took place in that moment that two strangers shared. I was told that while I was in the hospital members of her family would come to see me every time they came to see their child who had been badly injured in the wreck.

But God was still not finished redeeming the damage done from that accident, one of His greatest lessons was about to unfold. While at home recuperating there was an incident that happened in the life of a young lady who lived across the street from us. She had gotten involved in the drug culture and had run away from home with one of her friends. She babysat for us and we had developed a relationship with her. We knew some of the things she was involved in but when we tried to warn her parents, we were accused of being too religious and told not to interfere. This brought home to us the need for a ministry not only to her but for other teenagers in the area. Something had to be done. My husband and I decided to start a "coffee house and bible study" in our home. It was discouraging at first but with a lot of prayer it grew. We had up to 35 teenagers in our living room, down the hall, and into the kitchen on any given night. Most of them came from our area but they also came from the city. The young lady across the street from us only came once or twice in the beginning but did not continue. But had it not been for her and her struggles, we would not have started what turned out to be a wonderful ministry.

The teenagers who came were hungry and we had plenty of spiritual food to share with them. When we were not leading the group, we invited pastors from several local churches to come and share. The kids were so open to the move of the Spirit and to what God wanted to teach them. It was not church as usual. There was lots of prayer and many of them would join in. Phil played the guitar and I helped lead worship songs, complete with hand motions. [One of the best parts is that the kids did not have cell phones back then with the ability to take videos.] It was, at least on my part, a joyful noise. It was awesome.

Those who came helped us make plans for a coffee house. We built a stage against the back of our house and had live Christian music, praise, spirited-filled messages, and testimonies all over loudspeakers. Our backyard yard had a small but natural amphitheater and it would be filled with people. No neighbor ever complained. It lasted about three wonderful years with several of the kids going into ministry themselves.

[Many years later one of those teenagers became my grandson's Sunday School teacher. One day, she told the class that she was going to teach them a song that had been taught to her by the grandparents of one of the students in that class, complete with hand motions.]

By the early 80's, our lives were rooted in the church. We were trying to learn how to walk in the Spirit and everything that comes along with that. At the time, we were just young enough and open enough to want it all. And then, the unthinkable happened. I found out that I had a disease called Thalassemia. It took a while before I learned I would not die from this condition because of its similarity to Sickle Cell Anemia. To say that I entered a time of confusion would be an understatement. This was the way I found out that the man I knew as my father growing up was not my biological father. [Who was my real family now? My brothers were only half-brothers. My grandparents on my father's side, Nanny and Pop, were not blood relatives. Who did I even look like? Was I going to die from this blood condition?] I cried a lot and became depressed. I decided to make the church my family and for the first time, I decided not to keep secrets from my close friends. But that decision caused a deep hurt in me. We had developed a loving relationship with the pastor and his wife, or so I thought.

The pastor's wife confronted me and told me that my problem was that I was clinging to my friends. That included her and the pastor which she felt was not a good thing. While there may have been some truth in that, she did not mean it in a helpful way. The revelation that who I thought was my father had been a lie was all too new to receive her words. [The power that words can hold is huge and we often use them without thinking what they may mean to the person hearing then.] I pulled back into my shell and found this hurt was another battlefield. I needed to be well armed. (Ephesians 6:10 -18)

Slowly, I found answers that helped me get on solid ground again. The doctor helped me understand that I was not going to die. I only had Thalassemia Trait and that brought with it a life of being anemic. Only the full-blown condition brought death most likely before the age of 20. I was just a carrier. Through this, I learned why I had not been able to donate blood when I had tried in the past and been turned down each time. I was told, "you need it more than we do." Regardless of the comment made by the pastor's wife, my church family filled the void and showed me God's love and compassion. [The fact that I will always be anemic and have to keep an eye on that has hardly been a problem. God has given me an extra dose of energy (I am a bit hyper-active), so I don't even know I am anemic most of the time.]

CHAPTER

BATTLEFIELDS

As a counselor, I know that most of us have strongholds, lies we believe about ourselves, that keep us from being all we could be. We don't seem to be able to overcome them. They are perceived weaknesses or flaws that we can't seem to accept or let go. We are embarrassed or ashamed by them. I found it almost impossible to speak them out loud or to put them in the light where they lose their sting. [Maybe you can take just an honest look at yours. How can you win the battle? I have a couple strongholds that I struggle with still. Most are no longer a battle but more like a skirmish. One of my strongholds is built on a foundation of the perception that I lack intellectual abilities that others have. The insecurity that is attached to those beliefs were birthed in the abuses I experienced and things I was told, or not told, as a child. I don't remember ever being told how smart I was or had my abilities encouraged.] The strongholds in my life were strengthened by my academic struggles in school between what I could do and what others seemed to be able to do. I did not see myself as measuring up to the abilities of others. I seemed to have a very narrow vision.

I was not a good student, no matter how hard I tried. I passed my classes but it took blood, sweat, and tears. One of the lies that I believed was that everyone knew how I struggled and that they thought I was a bit dumb. That brought with it undeserved shame. I often felt like I was living a lie or pretending so others would not see my problem. Many times, I didn't try things for fear of failing. I brought some of that into my adulthood. Twice as an adult, I was offered opportunities that I sabotaged because it seemed safer to turn down the opportunity than to take on a challenge that I believed I could not do. One was to help with the design of the lobby of a hotel in town. The other, many years later, was connected to providing some graphic design and PR type work for a realtor. [I will never know if I could have done those jobs and that is something that I regret.]

My son seemed to suffer from the same things. He struggled in school and defaulted to thinking he couldn't which often earned him the title of "class clown" by some of his teachers. One day, he came home from school upset and told me he hated school. I think his struggles became more than he could handle. He was about fourteen years old and it was time we got him some help; something I needed but never received.

We were told by the principal of his school that there was testing that could be done at the Medical College of Virginia's Adolescent Learning Center, so we took advantage of it. The tests found that he had plenty of intelligence but he had problems with comprehension and retention. He had problems with reading a story but if I gave him a "Guinness World Book of Records" at bedtime, he shared little bits of information the next morning. We started setting up a more structured schedule. He was given medication and we made attempts at helping him take more pride in his appearance. He tried hard and the change was amazing. His grades soared but that brought a new problem. His teachers were not told of what was going on, only the principal. The doctors didn't want expectations to skew the results. Teachers started to make an example of him which caused his peer group to tease him. It embarrassed him and he started to stop his efforts including his medications. What his peers thought of him seemed more important than making good grades. A lesson many of us need to learn and change. Success is not a bad thing and neither is failing if you have tried your best but both can look scary, especially to a child.

Without knowing it, my son helped me to face up to my very similar stronghold. All this time, I watched him and remembered my struggle. I admired his efforts to change because I also understood the feeling of not being able to succeed in school academics. But for a long time,

I did not face my stronghold and I continued to believe the lies I had brought into my adulthood. It was his fight that forced me onto my own battlefield.

The first battle was finding out the truth about myself. I joined a group of women who were facing their own intellectual and memory weaknesses. It let me know that others fight the same battle and that there was nothing of which to be ashamed. It was just a part of who I was. I needed to find out what I could achieve if I worked at it and got the help I needed. After all, I had an example living with me every day of how we can change the path we are on; my son did that.

My son struggled all the way through school, but he grew into an accomplished, talented man who is a wonderful husband and father. [He works hard to provide what his family needs. He knows how to love them well. He is by any measure a success and remains an example to me. He is to be admired.]

God started me down a road of redeeming the lies I believed. I decided, with the help and encouragement of a number of friends, including my husband, to conquer one of my biggest fears. I took a college course to see if I could achieve what my son had done. I wanted to know once and for all if I was as "stupid" as I had believed for so long.

One of my good friends was in graduate school at Virginia Commonwealth University (VCU). She went with me to find the location of my first class so I would not get lost trying to find it on the first day of school and become anxious and fearful from the get-go. We went into where the class was to be held and picked out a seat close to the front but not too close; we sat down. No one else was in the room and I started to cry. I felt the same fear I later felt standing in front of that podium shaking the day I shared my shame for the first time with the women's group. I wondered why I was doing this. [Was it too late to run?] But I knew in my spirit that if I did not do this now, I never would. If I were to win this battle, the time to step onto the battlefield was now.

I found out that VCU offered testing for students and I took advantage of that soon after I entered. The result...I was found to have plenty of intelligence but problems with comprehension and retention. [The same as my son.] They called it a "minimal brain dysfunction." [Today, I think it would be ADD or ADHD.] I was given a letter that allowed me to take more time on tests if I needed it. That eliminated a lot of stress by helping me relax some and not be overly affected by test anxiety. I knew I could learn, but I needed to find new ways of learning; ways, I had never figured out as a child from resources I didn't know were available. [Today finding out about these problems and how to help them is almost taken for granted.] But I figured it out on my own without medication. I claimed 2 Timothy 2:15 ("Study thyself approved unto God, a workman that need not to be ashamed...") as my motivation verse and I needed it for the next seven years.

In algebra, I used memorization along with the help of my friend who was in grad school and who could do the algebra I was trying to learn in her head. I often wondered "how does she do that?" Also, I combined logic and extra time to figure out the multiple-choice questions. I worked through all the problems and then went back to the ones I couldn't figure out and started to plug in the multiple choice answers one at a time until I found the one that worked. [Wonder if you would call that cheating?] I hope not.

For subjects that required knowing facts like biology, history, statistics, etc., I used color coding while studying to help me have a visual memory of which facts were part of a particular subject. I put all the facts about 1492 in red and facts about Columbus in blue. I was able to go back to the material associated with each color and saw the facts connected to that color. That worked well with essay answers. I also took copious notes in class paying special attention to the way the professor emphasized some things or repeated other things. This gave me an idea of what was important to the professor and what was most likely to be on a test. Then, I read the material after class concentrating on the parts of the material the professor seemed to think were important. As a slow reader, I didn't have the greatest ability to retain what I read. I only read what I needed to retain. I knew this was not cheating. I thought it was being smart.

However, English was different and easier for me. It was a lot of writing and I liked to write. Expressing my thoughts and telling stories about the things I had experienced in my life and in the lives of my friends or acquaintances came easy to me. I found that the English professor liked my work and more than once read my assignment to the class. That was embarrassing but I loved it!

It took a lot of work during those seven years of undergrad and sometimes it caused me a lot of frustration because of my lack of faith in myself, but it worked. I graduated with a Bachelor of Science degree (Cum Laude) in journalism and a minor in psychology. At the time, I had no idea that God would take me into counseling. When I got a taste of how it works and what is used in helping folks with mental health problems, I found that many of the principles fit perfectly with the principles that Jesus taught in the Bible. "Do no harm" was the rule/ ethic of the day. [I think the Lord likes that goal.] I found that a lot of the materials and modalities taught in my psychology classes sounded similar. It seemed to me that many of the authors of the material started with the same premise used in other materials. But they tweaked what they wrote by adding new concepts or perspectives turning them into a different modality. [There really isn't "anything new under the sun (Son)."]

It took quite a while to get to that counseling degree. I had started as an undergraduate student in 1987 at the age of 41 with the idea that I would be a journalist. I liked to write but had ruled out English because the volume of reading required didn't fit with my problems with comprehension and retention. I graduated in 1994 only to find out that being a journalist had some problems. It required long hours, covering stories in bad parts of town whenever the story "broke." Not what I had in mind. For a few years, I took a job teaching OSHA compliance courses to workers who worked with hazardous materials and needed to be certified before they could do the work. Interesting... but again not what I had in mind.

A few years later, God prompted me through my husband and a friend who showed me a way to seek a degree in counseling that was not offered on the VCU campus, instead it was downtown at MCV/ VCU. God gave me very clear directions my first semester in graduate school. It was a vision of what God wanted me to do with my training, but He left out some important instructions in the beginning. He made it clear that I would be combining my secular training and my spiritual experience with healing prayer in a ministry. He told me I had to do 3 things before He would show me the specifics of the vision. 1) I had to graduate from the Counseling program. 2) I had to find a job and complete the 4,000 hours of supervised training required for Licensure (completed by working at a mental health clinic for 5 years). 3) I had to pass the State Licensure exam.

When I had finished all of that, He was good to His word. It became clear that I was to start a faith based, non-profit counseling agency which had the mission of working with those who were financially challenged and who did not have insurance. It was to be a 10 year ministry. I was to see anyone; with insurance or without insurance. I provided a very broad sliding scale but required people pay something if at all possible. I only had to turn two people away in 10 years because I simply did not have the resources that they needed. It was a privilege to serve these folks and the Lord blessed me and my ministry in so many ways during that time. I knew that it was a ministry straight from God and I loved it.

God knew a long time before I did what I would end up doing. Looking back, it was such a logical direction for me to take. I learned to love what I do professionally and it was a path that fit very well with ministering to folks who found themselves in difficult situations and who were helped by both the world of secular education and Holy Spirit training.

God had redeemed me from a lifetime of believing a lie. I was able to finish college with honors. [Thanks, son] I was not stupid after all. The degree was awesome, but what I learned about who I really was and how that area of my life was being redeemed was priceless.

CHAPTER

STRONGHOLDS

The other stronghold in my life, aside from not believing that I was a good student, was the fear around intimacy that had developed as I grew up. [It is hard to talk about. While it has gotten weaker, it has never left me completely. At this point, I have doubts that it ever will.] In counseling clients, I have seen people who suffer in this area. Some succeeded in overcoming it but most learn to understand what is going on. However, that does not always make the symptoms go away.

[One can experience strong, spontaneous, physical reactions for a long time and sometimes they never go away. Sometimes body memories linger and it can transport oneself back to the time of the abuse. The person can be triggered by a touch, a smell, or a memory causing one to "feel" the same way they did when the abuse occurred By the end of WWI and WWII, this phenomenon was called "shell shock" but treatment was new and not the best. Now the medical and mental health communities have a name for this, Post Traumatic Stress Disorder (PTSD). [Treatment has come a long way. But it remains very hard to treat because of the nature of the disorder.]

Is it my "thorn in my flesh" as Paul talks about? (2 Corinthians 12:6-7) And will it remain and continue to cause me more grief? Is it a lack of faith in me? Do I really believe that God intends to or can break this stronghold? Or am I supposed to just accept it? Whatever the reason, it seems that I have chosen, after a long battle, the latter. It feels like a default setting in my life. I can't switch off the emotions of it, so I will just accept it as a facet of who I am. I don't like it. I do believe deep inside that God can change the default settings.

What I did not know as I grew up is how the experiences in my life would affect me as an adult. I did not understand things like "body memories, insecurities, or the effects of Post-Traumatic Stress Disorder." I developed problems with intimacy that I fought with counseling, prayer, confession, and lots of tears. I thought I was winning the battle for a long time and then a crisis in my life created more stress than I could handle.

The crisis began when my mother developed throat cancer. Her cancer battle was simultaneous with my undergraduate educational challenges in college. I needed a lot of emotional and physical strength to get through my classes. Often, I took my school work to the hospital and she seemed to take pleasure in knowing that one of her children would be a college graduate. However, she did not live to see that.

The road that led to her death was long and very painful for her. As I watched her fight her own battle, I struggled with how to walk through it with her. The memories created throughout my life by her came to the forefront of my mind many times. Compassion mingled with anger making it hard for me to accept the role of caring daughter, one more time. The fact that my mom was not drinking during this time meant that the good part of her was always near the surface. I did not have the strength it took to handle her dying, my memories and regrets over our relationship, and also do the work it took to complete school and fight against the feelings of failure I felt because of my struggles with intimacy. Not to mention, the guilt I felt in my marriage because I was a Christian wife and should have been able to accept healing and have the faith to believe. [Funny how you forget the things you believe and live by when the crisis gets bad enough.] It was not a good time in my life.

My mother knew she was dying and so did I. Her pain was so bad that they let her have control over her pain; she decided when to push some pain medicine into her veins. In spite of the life she lived, she was a strong woman. If she knew someone was coming to visit, she would hold off on the medication so she was alert during their visit. One day when I went to visit her, she seemed to be more alert than usual. She called me to her bedside and gave me her wedding ring. We both knew what that meant. She knew that the end was very near. I left in tears and asked that the nurses please call me in time to be with her when she died. After that day, I changed the way I prayed for her. I prayed, "Lord if you are not going to heal her will you please take her?" I knew that she had become a Christian when she was young and had reaffirmed that when a friend of mine visited her. She died just a few days after she gave me her ring. One of my regrets was that the nurses did not call me in time to get there so as far as I know she died alone. [Something that I hope I don't have to do.]

God gave me a tender heart for her and what she was facing. Being with her every day in the hospital while she was dying was bathed with God's grace.

I tried to put up a good front, but this was one of the most difficult times in my life. Being on the battlefield and trying to fight the pain brought on by her death and my regrets caused me to lose some of my fight. I gave into feeling like I would never conquer my battle with intimacy and accepted that it would be my cross to bear. As a Christian I felt shame that I could not just "give that to God." Yet, I knew that God loves me just the way I am because He has proven that over and over.

I began to understand...what felt like failure in my life enabled me to have empathy and be able to show it to the women facing the same types of challenges who ended up sitting in my office. They sat across the room from me weeping because they felt a pain that does not go away. During this time, I visited my good friend who had helped me so much in school. I put my head in her lap and wept from that same kind of pain that feels like it will never go away. Because I know that kind of pain, I knew better how to comfort them with the comfort I have received. (2 Corinthians 1:3-4) [I know that I am loved by my heavenly father, by my husband, family and friends. And that is no small thing; it is part of His redeeming love for me and mine towards them.]

CHAPTER

ACCEPTING AND
SHOWING LOVE

So much of the healing that has taken place in my life has been because someone cared enough to show me what I had not seen growing up but I desired now. So many people around me showed me that kind of love and care. God used Betty and Jeff, our mentors and friends, to teach us. [I don't think that they knew that we considered them our mentors and would probably shun that title.] Jeff had gone to a bible college. He was an ordained pastor and an elder in our Baptist church. He was laid back and was very gentle in his approach to life. I heard him say several times, "If the Holy Spirit is in it you can share about peanut butter and the Lord can use it to bring people to Himself."

His passion was military aviation but he had bad eyes and they would not take him in the service. He went on to get his pilot's license and became very well known for his documenting the subject. He was able to fly in almost every plane the military made in order to write about them. He died prematurely while flying a World War II plane home from Oregon.

Betty, Jeff's wife, was the person that God used the most to break my shell. They were our age, maybe a little younger, but giants in the Lord as far as we were concerned. Betty was a missionary kid, raised for a good part of her life in Brazil. She had a big, warm, loving, boisterous, fun-loving Christian family and I loved everything about them. It did not take long for me to want to be like them but that required entering into a world of affection and that included physical touch. Something that I did not learn as a child and it scared me to death.

One day, I confessed to Phil that I wished I could show my affection back to Betty and tell her how much I cared for her. But every time I tried, the words came as far as my throat and got stuck there. At that he simply said "let's go." Of course, what he meant was we are going to see our friends. I sat without saying much all the way there. When we got to Betty and Jeff's house, we settled down into the usual separation of men in one room and the women in another. But this is not what my husband had in mind and the rooms were only separated by an island.

As Betty and I talked in the kitchen, a loud voice from the other room interrupted us. The voice of my impatient husband said, "Betty, Brenda has something to tell you." It was one of the hardest moments of my life. I had to say something, do something, and I didn't know how it would come out but I told her how much I cared for her and I remember the warm embrace that followed. I was in a safe place experiencing the love of Christ. [That is what safe affection should feel like from other people.]

In the years following that first expression of love that I struggled through, I became known as one of the best huggers in the church. It was like the little boy who had his finger in the hole in the dike holding back a wall of water. So much changed in that moment, that it felt like a flood that swept away years of misguided lessons I had learned. During that time, I learned as a child would learn to accept without question what God was doing. [There is beauty in the innocence of showing God's love.] This was an awesome kind of redemption in my life; learning to love, God's way.

Learning to love was the last part that I shared standing in front of that podium. As I closed my talk, I emphasized to the ladies that this may be the end of what I have to share today but it is not the end of my story. More importantly, it is not the end of your story either. God is not finished with any of us... He is still redeeming our lives. I know the women in the crowd that day were shocked to learn of what I had experienced but they affirmed me as they loved me with their embraces.

CHAPTER 12

CONFUSING MEMORIES

I would not want to leave you thinking that remembering the buried things in my life was completely a thing of the past. Not that long ago, in December 2019, I was attending a church luncheon. I had taken a good friend as my guest and we were listening to a woman tell her dynamic testimony. There was so much passion and joy as she shared her hurts and mistakes. It surprised me. It turned out to be one of the most unusual days of my life. So much of what she shared was similar to what I had experienced growing up.

Her story captured me. I was feeling her emotions as she told of her abuse and redemption. Then something reached inside of me when I was not expecting it and pulled out emotions from somewhere deep in my soul. The sadness in me was overwhelming! I did not understand it. I started to have glimpses of people I care for now or cared for in the past. I remembered... no I felt the pain in their lives as if it was happening in front of me that very moment. It was like it was happening to me too. I did not know how to react to the emotions that were unleashed in me so quickly. I wanted to weep but I wasn't ready to let that happen in front of over one hundred women. Meanwhile, women were up front praying for folks, but I did not go up. I didn't know what to say or how to explain it. So, I prayed that God would tell me what to do. My friend recognized my struggle and without a word reached out, took my hand, and I felt her comfort. I was calmed because I knew she understood my struggle but the sadness stayed.

Afterwards, just like the first time the memories came, I got busy. There were Christmas decorations to put up and cleaning to do but that only worked for a while. When I stopped, the tears would often start again. Then another memory came, one that I was almost too fearful to remember yet, it felt familiar as if this was not the first time I had this memory...one that was hard to even write down. I was young and in the same bed as my father and mother...a rare event in my life. It was all so vague and incomplete, but I remembered feeling a touch that did not feel right. This was a body memory. Even at my young age, I think I knew it wasn't right. Then the memory was gone. I don't remember that anything else happened.

[What does one do with something like that? It brings questions that can't be answered and feelings that can't be understood. Was it real? I'll never know. I don't want to believe it is true because as an adult I know what it might mean. But as a counselor, I know even if the memory comes from a child, we have to honor the thoughts and feelings that they have. But without further evidence presented, we are left with incomplete, vague emotions about what might have been that comes from unsubstantiated facts. But I wondered out of that memory, if it was real, how could God create redemption? (Romans 5:3-5) And, if it was not real, how would I ever know how to deal with it? I hardly think about it now, so that in itself is healing. God doesn't waste anything in our lives but it is up to us to seek Him and see what He can do with the worst events in our lives.]

CLOSING NOTE

I know that having memories of the experiences in my past both good and bad will probably show up once in a while. After all, I have had quite a few years to collect them in the recesses of my mind. They don't affect me the way they used to and usually do not stay long with me. Maybe, that is what comes from seeing that I can be healed from the pain of the hurtful events that happened even if the memories keep coming. (1 Peter 4:12-13)

Also, I have matured to the point of being able to incorporate so many of those events into what God has for me now and in the future. I have learned that I can use those events and the pain from them to encourage, teach, and show love to many with whom I have a relationship. I have learned the value of letting others that I trust into that pain when I just can't handle it alone. Most of the shame is gone because I have been able to share or put in the light the dark times in my life. That has been and is healing for my soul.

At the beginning of *My Story* I quoted something from a book by

John Bradshaw that sums up what I have and am learning from my life. It is worth repeating.

"I began to see that shame is one of the major destructive forces in all human life. In naming shame I began to have power over it."

What now? I have so many things I am looking forward to doing with the rest of this life as God gives it to me. Will I do them all? I doubt it...because I keep adding to my "bucket list." Will I do them all the way the Lord would have me do them? I doubt it...because I am an imperfect vessel that He has chosen for some reason that I am yet to understand. I have weaknesses that I have not been able to overcome. I am not the most intellectual person in the world, but I seem to have been given a lot of wisdom from what I have walked through. And, what I lack in intellect He has given to me through my relationships with some very, spiritual, mature, and intellectual friends. What they may lack He has given to me many times through the gift of His Holy Spirit.

I started this book to make sure that my family knew parts of my life that I doubt they knew before. It has become a labor of love for me and for them. Its main purpose is to glorify God and to give Him the credit for the healing and love He has poured into me. And it is hopeful that whoever reads it will know that God does "restore the years the locust has eaten" Joel 2:25a. He has a ministry of redemption. (And I now know, without a doubt, that God redeems the events in our lives that cause us pain).

This story will never end but now seems a good place to stop writing.

"The confidence of my calling enables me to overcome every difficulty without shame, for I have an intimate revelation of this God. And my faith in him convinces me that he is more than able to keep all that I've placed in his hands safe and secure until the fullness of his appearing."

2 Timothy 1:12

The Passion Translation

EPILOGUE

I ended my story on a Friday in June, 2020, with this statement: "This story will never end but now seems a good place to stop writing." That was true until the following Monday when I received an email from a woman I have never met, but I have had communication with her in the past. Whether or not you believe that "life is about Gods timing," you must admit that what unfolded after the email was received, just two days after I "finished," was remarkable timing. I realized that I had better pay a little more attention to what was happening.

This woman and I were drawn together through a series of events about a year prior through Ancestory.com. Her family had been looking into Ancestory.com for family connections and somehow my name had come up. So, she reached out to me by looking up my name on the internet and finding my business information. She thought we were related. I recognized the name she gave me as my biological father's name. I certainly had not let anyone know that name. She and her family seemed to have a head start emotionally in coming to grips with the "truth" of it all. But it was just too much for me to take in and too much to believe. Being talented at putting off and hiding facts which are hard to face or examine, I did not seek to look too deeply at the evidence at hand. So once again I brought out the same "box" I had put the 67 memories in some time ago and put this new information in it.

After talking and sharing information that we both had, it strongly suggested that a member of her family was indeed my biological father. I felt some of the same feelings as I did the day my mother called and told me, "your father is not your father." I wanted not to believe what this woman was sharing with me. I didn't want to step outside my comfortable area of belief into another world full of questions, many without answers. After all, at my age what difference did it make? I didn't think it would change anything and it might cause renewed pain. I was not interested in enduring that again. After a while, I didn't think about it very much and soon I regained a position in my comfort zone. But God has a way of showing us things which we are not looking for, things we need to know or should know in order to know His truth in the many situations in our lives. He does not seem to have much interest in our "comfort zones."

The email I had received that Monday morning included pictures of who she believed was my biological father, and like it or not I had to start seriously considering this was true. I saw the email while I was at work between clients and not ready or willing to look at the pictures at that time. But there he was, and I could not just ignore him. She wanted to send me more but I knew I couldn't handle seeing more. Just like I knew I could not handle the *67 Memories* that day in my yard. I asked her to hold off on sending any more pictures right away, that now was not a good time, and I needed more time to process what was happening. She seemed to understand and graciously said she would wait to hear from me if and when I wanted to see more.

I had thirty minutes before my next client, so I did the only thing I knew to do. I reached out to three of my closest friends who I knew would pray for me. When my clients came I was able to focus on them and their issues, not my problems. My sessions went well and I called that grace but I had to decide what to do about calling the woman who had sent me the pictures. I had to make a decision about what to do. Do I just say, "no thank you, I am not interested" or do I open up to what I may find if I let this woman into my life; past, present and future?

Before I called her back I needed to at least look at the pictures. Maybe I would have a "light bulb moment," an epiphany moment, and I would hear God telling me exactly what to do and how to do it. Things seldom seem to work that way. I looked and cried. One moment I wanted this man and this family to be mine, the next I was scared to face the fact that it may not be my biological father. What should I do with all the emotions inside that had been stirred up? If I explore all the pieces of this puzzle, would it lead me to how God is going to redeem this part of my history, my life?

I am surprised by how many puzzle pieces to this story have been found offering insights that need to be considered. I wonder if it will ever stop. I am hearing names I have never heard and stories that seem to be unrelated to me. But with each thing this woman shares, I find myself starting to believe. And the more I believe, the more I am drawn into the story of a family I don't know but think I should. I can understand more how others feel when life surprises hit them and the hardest decision is "do I or don't I."

I have stayed in contact with the woman (1st cousins we think) many times by email, text, and phone calls. She has sent me a wealth of information about names, the history of the family, her life, stories, and pictures of her two little girls. The picture she sent of herself reminds me of myself at her age. I have grown fond of her and feel certain we will meet face to face one day in the near future. The fact that this man she presents to me as my father seems likely to be just that. It is an experience I was not prepared for, but God seems to be determined for me to examine all the puzzle pieces that are coming my way. Perhaps, He has plans to reveal to me something I have never been able to figure out. Who is my real family, where are they, and what are they like? It no longer frightens me but gives me reason to experience new relationships and create some new memories. Time will tell.

God seems to be pouring new things into my life so fast I can hardly process them. A family member came to me and wanted to talk to me about something concerning my stepfather that added curiosity and stirred up anxiety in me. I couldn't use my old practice of putting it in a "box" to look at later; that didn't work at this point, the "box" was getting too full.

Shortly after finishing the first draft of my story, I gave copies to some family members and one of my sons came to me and said, "I have to tell you something about Johnny,"(my step father) but he could not talk at that time. After he left, my thoughts bounced all over the place. I did not get the feeling at the time from the way it was said that it was a good thing and I began to think terrible things. Being a counselor did not help either; as counselors we hear so many stories of abuse and see so many hurting people suffering from what someone else has done to them that we sometimes have to fight to stay positive and to not jump to conclusions. Thoughts of what might be mingled with thoughts of what was real in the past events of my life. It was almost inevitable that my thoughts would try to think the worst.

For once I did not want to tuck the possible memories that he had into a box, but I had little choice. It was his memory and his decision about when to share it. Two months went by before I would find out what memory he had hidden in his secret box. He came by to check on his father who had had some minor surgical procedures done and while we talked he opened his box of hidden memories. He let us into the secret he had been keeping for 40 years. As he told his story, I could not believe what I was hearing and it took me back to the time I had experienced the same feelings and reactions he was telling us about.

When my kids were young they would often stay with my mother and her husband in their mobile home. I never heard a negative word from any of the children about going there and nor did any of them ever resist going to stay with Grandma and Johnny Buck, as they called them. I generally would listen carefully to the things that they shared when they came home because of the things I saw growing up. I knew there was drinking in their history but assumed things were much better because the kids shared some wonderful times they had with them during their visits. They did not share the kind of stories that usually accompanied drinking. When he finished telling us the story, I asked if it could be shared. He told me that he was not ashamed and he did not mind what others might think.

His memories were triggered by two "memories" that I shared in my story. They made him think about what happened to him when he was about ten years old. They were tied together, but are different. The first one was about how passive and non-violent Johnny always seemed to be. He compared the way he felt about Johnny to when he read about when I came down stairs one morning, when I was about ten, to find my mother beaten and her face bruised, bloody with Johnny just standing across the room not doing or saying anything. My son said to us, "Mom, that is the way I saw him; passive." But my son had realized that was not the way Johnny was all the time. The second story caused reactions in me that I can't explain; it brought up anger, shame, guilt, and sorrow all at the same time and I did not want to feel or exhibit them. I could not do anything about what happened to my son but feel sorry that it had happened.

My son stayed with Grandma and Johnny Buck. He had been playing outside for a while and when he came in he found his grandparents fighting. He said, "I have never seen so much anger and hate in anyone's face like Johnny had on his." He continued, "He was yelling at her and she was pushing back. She told him that she was going to call the police and grabbed the phone. He grabbed the cord and a knife and with one swing, cut the cord. I grabbed the knife out of his hand and pointed it at him and told him if he hurt my grandmother I was going to kill him. He just looked down at me and with a smirk on his face, laughed a small laugh and left the house." When he finished telling his secret it felt like the breath had been sucked out of the room. All I could say was "I am so sorry...why didn't you tell me?"

Then my mind went back to my own event when I pointed a knife at Henry and said, "leave or I will kill you." My son's story mirrored mine in so many ways and I silently asked myself, "why didn't you tell?" How close we both came to scarring our lives forever. As children were we brave or stupid? Did we act out of love or hate? All my life I thought my answer to that was hate. "He was the only person I ever hated," I would often say. But now, I am not sure. We both wanted to protect someone we loved. For me, it was my mother and for my son, it was his grandmother. We were both trying to protect the same person. I wondered how many times had my mother and Johnny fought with her being the loser? I will never know. So many secrets based in shame.

How can God redeem these two memories so tied together in time? I have talked with wise friends, professional friends, and pondered this with God. I don't know the full answer yet, but I am starting to see ways something good can come out of these memories and it will not take a rocket scientist or a psychiatrist to figure it out. The answer is found in the sharing of it. The sting is taken away when trust and empathy are built by having the opportunity to share what is hidden. Many of my battles have been won and the victory-prize is my redemption.

"I don't depend on my own strength to accomplish this; however I do have one compelling focus: I forget all of the past as I fasten my heart to the future instead. I run straight for the divine invitation of reaching the heavenly goal and gaining the victory-prize through the anointing of Jesus."

Philippians 3:13-14 The Passion Translation

One last thing that needs to be mentioned before I close...

What about all the events that seem to have no reasons or emotional end to them? The other day, I opened up Facebook and the first thing that popped up was a post from a member of my father's family (the man I knew as my father growing up). It was a sweet memory of something she remembered about her dad. I had a rush of emotion that was a mixture of anger, jealousy, hurt, sadness, and regret. It brought back what I did not have growing up but what I always wanted. But it didn't last, I could feel the good that they had experienced that left them with warm memories of him and that is a good thing and it is healing.

There is a verse that is one of my "go to" verses when I am confused or don't understand. I stand on this verse, maybe you can too.

"The secret things belong to the Lord our God,

but the things revealed belong to us

and to our children forever..."

Deuteronomy 29:29

GALLERY

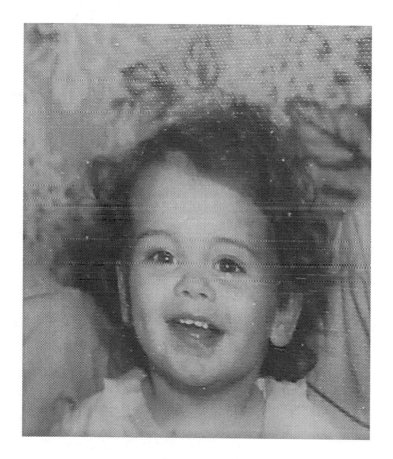

picture age 1

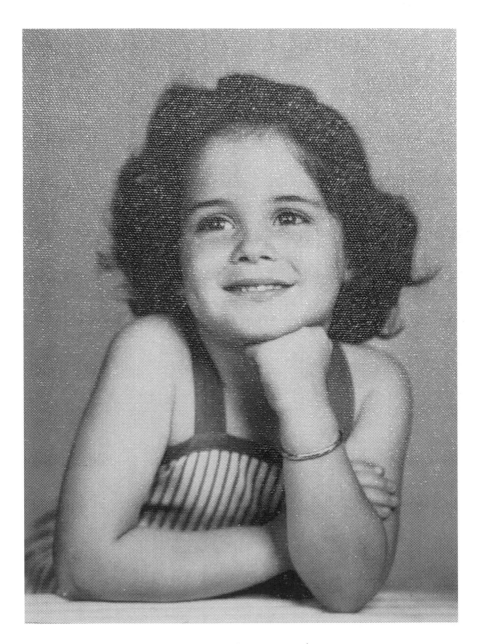

contest winner age 4

Brenda about 9

Brenda about 10 in raincoat

mom and dad and 1ˢᵗ son at Big daddys house 1942

Big Daddys house now

Phil and Brenda 1970

Printed in the United States
By Bookmasters